INTRO

This version of the Stations of the Cross focuses on persons with disabilities, and on those who may be homebound or chronically ill, and their families. We all have disabilities of a sort, whether it is poor vision and we need eyeglasses, or we have a chronic but manageable disease, or we have a broken leg that impairs us temporarily. Not all persons with disabilities suffer pain or are ill, but they all may find life difficult and challenging from time to time; they may suffer workplace discrimination or bullying or find everyday tasks difficult. Jesus purposely let himself be disabled on the cross and has forever united himself in love and hope to those with disabilities.

The Stations of the Cross presented here may be used by individuals or in a group setting such as a nursing home, hospital, or parish. If using these stations in a group setting, a leader could be selected and may announce each station and lead the group in the traditional opening: "We adore you O Christ and we bless you, for by your holy cross you have redeemed the world." The leader will read the reflection, and then all may recite the station's prayer together.

Stepping off...

If you are praying these stations by yourself, begin by putting yourself in a relaxed position. Close your eyes for a moment and gather your thoughts. Let God fill your heart. Picture yourself on a rural dusty road. You see a busy town just ahead. You have heard of a healer who is visiting, and you have traveled a long way to meet him. You are in need of his healing hands, and he is in need of a traveling companion. Jesus meets you on the edge of the town and invites you to journey with him to Calvary. He warns you the road may be rough but full of wonders at the end. You begin the journey of the cross together in hope and love.

TWENTY-THIRD PUBLICATIONS *A division of Bayard*
1 Montauk Avenue, Suite 200 • New London, CT 06320 • (860) 437-3012 or (800) 321-0411 • www.twentythirdpublications.com
ISBN 978-1-62785-418-4 •
Printed in the U.S.A. • Cover photo: © iStockphoto.com / Racide

The First Station

Jesus is condemned to death

We adore you, O Christ,
and we bless you,
For by your holy cross
you have redeemed the world.

When we receive bad news, our lives can be turned upside down. We may receive a devastating diagnosis, lose a job or our home, or learn of a loved one's passing. We can feel very alone in our grief and our suffering and may even feel abandoned by God as we struggle to cope with what life brings us. God is still there, but we cannot always see him in the darkness. When we suffer, God, our Father, sees that we are about to enter into a journey full of unknowns that may lead us to question our very self and the purpose of our being. God suffers when we suffer.

Our Father would like us to join his Son as he begins his own journey of suffering. Jesus has just received the news that

he is to be condemned to death. Jesus feels very alone as one by one his followers leave him and deny him. Jesus knows we may be experiencing unbearable situations too, and he invites us to walk with him, for he knows that his pain and suffering will have a purpose, and our suffering will too. Our pain, whether in the body or mind, real or imagined, joins us to Christ's own suffering, thus bringing us closer to him. Let us now walk together on the road to Calvary sharing our struggles, our pains, and our love as hope awaits us on the cross.

As Jesus begins his journey to Calvary, we pray for all those beginning their own journeys of worry, anxiety, and suffering.

The Second Station

JESUS CARRIES HIS CROSS

We adore you, O Christ,
and we bless you,
For by your holy cross
you have redeemed the world.

The cross is heavy, rough, and splintered. It is awkward and long. Can any one person carry it? Jesus accepts the challenge of carrying the cross; it is the first step of his journey, a path that will be difficult and full of anguish and will result in his death. But Jesus accepts his cross willingly and with purpose, for he knows the journey will bring new hope to many. He picks up his cross with determination and invites us to do the same.

Life can bring us situations that are more than we can handle. In these times, God offers us a cross to bear. When we accept our crosses to carry, we ask ourselves, "Will we be

able to carry the cross and bear the burden and the suffering? Will we be able to go the distance and complete the journey to the end? Can we do it alone?" Jesus is alone in bearing his own cross, but as we walk with him, bearing our own crosses, we find ourselves with a lighter load. As Jesus carries the weight of his cross, we find his love helping us to carry ours. Jesus is always walking with us, helping us with our difficulties, our sorrows, our pains, and our cross, even as he carries his own.

WE ACCOMPANY AND PRAY FOR ALL THOSE WHO LIVE WITH DISABILITIES, AND THOSE WITH A CHRONIC OR TERMINAL ILLNESS. MAY THEY HAVE THE COURAGE TO ASK JESUS TO HELP THEM TO CARRY THEIR CROSS.

The Third Station

JESUS FALLS FOR THE FIRST TIME

We adore you, O Christ,
and we bless you,
For by your holy cross
you have redeemed the world.

Carrying our cross may feel overwhelming. The cross is extremely heavy and awkward to carry. We may think we cannot go on. We stumble and fall, praying that the weight of the cross, our tears, and our distress don't crush us before we reach the end of our journey. We take a rest, and we see that Jesus has stumbled too. We close our eyes and pray that we may find the strength to get back up and continue on. When we open our eyes and gaze into Jesus' face, we are filled with a renewed energy to continue, and we arise.

When we are in distress or struggling in life, we often stumble and fall. Sometimes it is difficult enough just getting up

off the ground. We can choose to stay on the ground if we are too afraid to go on, or we may choose to get up and run away from the cross, but neither of these choices will end our difficulties and struggles in life. Only by finishing our walk with Jesus will we find hope and new life. Jesus encourages us to pick up our cross so we may resume our journey together. We continue on with renewed strength and resolve, fueled by the love of Christ.

WE PRAY FOR THOSE WHO HAVE STUMBLED UNDER THE WEIGHT OF THEIR CROSS AND MAY BE TOO AFRAID TO GO ON. MAY OUR LOVE STRENGTHEN THEM AND GIVE THEM HOPE TO CONTINUE THE ROAD TO CALVARY.

The Fourth Station

JESUS MEETS HIS MOTHER

We adore you, O Christ,
and we bless you,
For by your holy cross
you have redeemed the world.

Jesus sees his mother in the crowd. Their eyes meet. If Mary could carry her son's cross, she would. Jesus' mother feels her son's pain. When we struggle in life or are suffering great pain, our family members want to help ease our burdens. They feel helpless at times as they watch their loved ones struggle with burdens no one should have to bear: a mother watches her newborn undergo multiple surgeries to correct congenital deformities; a father watches a daughter learn to walk again after an auto accident; a grandma sneaks a fifty dollar bill to her grandson, who just lost a job due to discrimination. Our families are also hurting, carrying their own

crosses while trying to carry ours as well.

When Jesus gazes into Mary's face, he lets his mother's love touch his heart so he may carry on. Our families share our pain, and they encourage us to continue on. We gain inner strength from their love, as well as from Mary, Mother of God, as we travel the long road to Calvary.

We pray for all families supporting loved ones who are struggling with the difficulties of life, especially those with disabilities or suffering in pain. May we find the strength to help them carry their cross.

The Fifth Station

SIMON OF CYRENE HELPS JESUS CARRY THE CROSS

We adore you, O Christ,
and we bless you,
For by your holy cross
you have redeemed the world.

Jesus finds he can no longer carry the full weight of his cross without collapsing. He can no longer carry the weight alone. Like Jesus, we all carry burdens that threaten to overwhelm us: a mother learns her child has committed a violent crime; a teenager learns he has cancer; a soldier learns she is now an amputee; a single father of five is forced to leave his job after being addicted to opioids. No one of us should walk this journey alone. We have friends and loving strangers to help us to carry on. We share in bearing each other's crosses. Sometimes we need someone to help us, and other times we can help another. Oftentimes, we find helping to carry

another's cross lightens our own.

Simon of Cyrene eases Jesus' burden by helping him to carry his cross. Simon shares his strength and his heart with Jesus, and Jesus is uplifted. And, in turn, Jesus helps us to carry our cross to Calvary.

WE PRAY WE WILL BE OPEN TO HELPING THOSE WHO NEED OUR HELP AND OUR HEARTS, AND WE PRAY THAT WE WILL ALLOW OTHERS TO HELP US WHEN WE, OURSELVES, CANNOT GO ON.

The Sixth Station

VERONICA WIPES THE FACE OF JESUS

We adore you, O Christ,
and we bless you,
For by your holy cross
you have redeemed the world.

This journey Jesus is on is a difficult one and involves much blood, sweat, and tears. Sometimes the burdens and pains we carry are too much, and we allow tears to flow from our eyes. We may be crying for what could have been, what is to come, or simply from the stress and distress we are currently experiencing. Tears are our way of showing others we need understanding and compassion. It is the simple kindness and compassion of others that will carry us through hurtful times.

Veronica, taking out a cloth, helps to give Jesus strength in one simple loving gesture of wiping away the sweat and tears from his face. This was a small, simple act of love and compas-

sion that can be huge to those who are saddened or suffering. Veronica was a stranger to Jesus who may have never known how much her simple act was appreciated. When we are carrying our crosses let us not be afraid to open our hearts and let the tears flow. Jesus and Veronica will be walking with us to wipe away our sweat and our tears. If our tears should fall to the ground, others will pick them up and carry them in their hearts.

We pray that we have the strength to look at pain in the faces of others and to offer them a small sign of compassion. We will offer a loving smile or helping hand, which will go a long way in lifting a suffering heart.

The Seventh Station

JESUS FALLS FOR THE SECOND TIME

We adore you, O Christ,
and we bless you,
For by your holy cross
you have redeemed the world.

The journey of life that we travel together is full of detours, potholes, and rocky ground. When we are given a cross to bear, our lives take a detour into unknown territory where we may not be able to see the path ahead and are unable to see the potholes that trip us or the boulders that block our path. We find the ground beneath us is no longer familiar and is difficult to walk on. We try to keep our balance and find our way back to the familiar and safe life we had before we were given a cross to bear. Often, however, we fall while trying to move forward. We fall and try to get back up to carry on. We know we cannot stay in the unfamiliar place where we have

fallen but must get up and keep going.

We look to Jesus to light a path for our footsteps, because he has walked this way before us. In that light we find encouragement, and we notice, for the first time, flowers along the sides of the road full of color and life, encouraging us to keep going so that we may walk on in hope.

We pray for all those who find themselves on new, unfamiliar roads and stumble and fall. We pray that they arise again with a renewed strength, for we know Jesus is with them now and always.

The Eighth Station

Jesus meets the women of Jerusalem

We adore you, O Christ,
and we bless you,
For by your holy cross
you have redeemed the world.

While we carry our crosses for the most part alone, we do find people along the way wanting to support us and cheer us on. Sometimes, however, those closest to us become overwhelmed with empathy and compassion. They sense our pain and feel the weight of our burdens, and these become crosses for them to bear. On his way to Calvary Jesus takes a moment to say a few words to the women of Jerusalem. He sees his distress reflected in their eyes, and he gives them comfort as they weep for him. In a turnabout way, the person suffering and in most need of comforting can reassure others that what is to come is meant to be and all will be well at the end of the road.

In this life, we are here for each other. We share our joys, our tears, our hopes, and our fears. In the midst of it all, God is ready to be our strength, our healer, and our hope. He will send us the people we need when our energies are waning. Let them into your heart and allow the love of Christ to fill your spirit anew.

We pray for the people around us who share our worries, burdens, and pain. May they find comfort in our Lord's assurances that all will be as it should be.

The Ninth Station

Jesus falls the third time

We adore you, O Christ,
and we bless you,
For by your holy cross
you have redeemed the world.

When we are diagnosed with a serious disease or find ourselves seriously impaired due to injury or disability, we embark on a journey, carrying a heavy cross. It will take time before we learn how to best carry our cross. We will fall, not just once or twice but several times. Each time we fall and get up again, we know there is the possibility that we will fall again. We worry that we may not get back up after the next stumble. We begin to feel tired and worn out as we watch Jesus fall for the third time.

Jesus falls, but he is not worried about getting back up. His Father gives him the strength to carry on, for his Son has not

yet reached his destination. With the Father and Son's help, we get back up and pick up our cross once again. We may stumble and fall many times, but Jesus will always be there to pick us up and carry us when we cannot go on.

We pray for all who are ill and in pain and feel that they cannot go on. We will help them back up to their feet to carry on and, with Jesus, we will walk with them to complete their journey.

The Tenth Station

JESUS IS STRIPPED OF HIS GARMENTS

We adore you, O Christ,
and we bless you,
For by your holy cross
you have redeemed the world.

Jesus is stripped of his last remnant of dignity. Our clothing is our last refuge. There is no more hiding our trials and tribulations from the eyes of others. Often when we enter hospitals and doctors' offices we are asked to give up our clothing, our dignity. We feel helpless and alone as we await an examination, surgery, or other medical procedure. We may feel as if we have lost our very identity. We have been carrying our cross for a while and we begin to feel the splintered wood in our hearts. We yearn to put on our favorite comfy clothes, put our feet up, and retreat to happier times. But, now, like Jesus, we have had our protective clothing stripped away and we feel exposed to the world. We patiently wait for news of our

health, and we wonder if we are nearing the end of our journey toward a cure—or the continuance of an uncertain future. Jesus is here, sharing our worries and anxiety, offering his love.

There may be other times when we have felt exposed and stripped of our dignity. We may have been teased on the playground for being different or stared at for looking different. We may have been shoved aside or ignored or been considered stupid by teachers or employers. Jesus is with us, even in those times when we feel most exposed to the cold hearts of others.

We pray for all who feel they are alone and exposed to harm. We will let them know they are not alone, that we are here, at their side, as are the Father, Son, and Holy Spirit.

The Eleventh Station

JESUS IS NAILED TO THE CROSS

We adore you, O Christ,
and we bless you,
For by your holy cross
you have redeemed the world.

In the ultimate act of sacrifice, Jesus allows himself to be disabled on the cross. Jesus, by being nailed to a tree, becomes a symbol for all those who are suffering, impaired, or incapacitated by mental or physical disabilities. Jesus must bear a great deal of pain and suffering before he reaches the end of his human life. Jesus even feels totally alone, abandoned by his Father. So often when we find ourselves disabled in one way or another or paralyzed by fear, we may feel abandoned by those who love us. If we are disfigured in any way, people may look away. If we are suffering, our loved ones may unintentionally shy away. If we have mental or behavioral disabilities, people

may become fearful and avoid us because we are different.

Jesus invites us to reflect upon disabilities in a new light. He is nailed to a cross on which he is paralyzed. He has lovingly allowed this to happen because it has a purpose. He wants us to know there is hope for all of us. We all have disabilities, some obvious, others hidden. We can be paralyzed by fear, worry, or anxiety. In all of this, Jesus, on the cross, gives us hope—hope in a new life and an end to all suffering and distress.

We pray for all those who are mentally or physically disabled or paralyzed by fear and distress. May they know we will not let them languish on their crosses alone.

The Twelfth Station

JESUS DIES ON THE CROSS

We adore you, O Christ,
and we bless you,
For by your holy cross
you have redeemed the world.

It is done. The suffering of Jesus has come to an end on the cross. The ultimate conclusion for those who are distressed or in pain is new life fueled by the love of Jesus and the hope in the resurrection.

If we allow Jesus to walk with us in life and accept his offer of support through his strength and love, our travels are made much easier. Death awaits each of us, but for those in great pain, death, when it comes, may be a relief. It is difficult to face death, whether it is our own or another's. When Jesus died, many of his followers grieved the loss of a friend, and the loss of hope, and the loss of the man. They did not yet know of the new life to come. They did not yet know Jesus the Christ would be breaking the chains of death. But we know the ending. We know Jesus suffered and died to give us hope in his resurrection. He gave us hope that, in the fullness of time, we too will be free of pain and all distress. This knowledge keeps us going on our own life's journey.

WE PRAY FOR ALL THOSE WHO HAVE RECENTLY PASSED AWAY; THEIR ANXIETIES AND SUFFERINGS HAVE ENDED. WE REACH OUT TO THOSE WHOSE PAIN AND GRIEF ARE JUST BEGINNING AND LET THEM KNOW THAT JESUS IS WITH THEM, HOLDING THEM IN THEIR GRIEF.

The Thirteenth Station

JESUS IS TAKEN DOWN FROM THE CROSS

We adore you, O Christ,
and we bless you,
For by your holy cross
you have redeemed the world.

Jesus' human life is over, his sufferings now ended, but there are still things to be done. His friends and family must still care for his body in a last loving act—preparation for his final resting place. When we pass away, our loved ones begin a new phase of their own journey of pain and suffering. Our cross is now lifted, but they are now picking up new crosses as they begin the grieving process. Going to the funeral home, contacting the church, picking out clothes for a burial, and procuring a final resting place are all things that must be done while carrying the cross of grief and accepting death. They try to look past their veil of tears to accomplish what they must do.

In our death, we join the Father, Son, Spirit, and communion of saints in heaven, helping to guide and protect our loved ones on earth. We know God will wipe away their tears and remind them that death is no more.

We pray for all those mourning the loss of loved ones. We will help them to carry heavy crosses of sorrow as they begin to grieve for their loved one.

The Fourteenth Station

JESUS IS LAID IN THE TOMB

We adore you, O Christ,
and we bless you,
For by your holy cross
you have redeemed the world.

The final task is burial. Jesus carried the cross to Calvary and died on the cross, and now must be laid to rest. He has been placed in the tomb and carefully, lovingly wrapped in linen. Our Catholic funeral rites are our final act of love for our loved ones. Their journey has ended, and now, we too, wrap them in linen, a pall, and we mourn together in a Mass. We share stories and laughter as we remember our loved one. We remember the crosses they bore and celebrate the new life they now share with our loving Father in heaven. We bring them to their final resting place and say our final goodbyes and promise to love them forever.

But is it really goodbye forever? In a few days the tomb of Jesus will be empty, as the bonds of death are broken. We are given hope in a new life, an eternal life with the Father, the Son, and Holy Spirit in heaven. We have faith that we will see our loved ones again, and that faith will give us the strength to carry our own crosses when we must. As one journey ends, another begins—as it has been from the beginning of time. The Father, Son, and Holy Spirit are always willing to help carry the load with their love.

We pray for all of us on earth today, those who are well and those who are suffering. May we find love, comfort, and hope in Christ Jesus, now and forever.

Closing Prayer

We are Wonderfully Made!

PSALM 139:1–5, 9–18

Lord, you have probed me, you know me:
you know when I sit and stand;
you understand my thoughts from afar.
You sift through my travels and my rest;
with all my ways you are familiar.
Even before a word is on my tongue, Lord,
you know it all.
Behind and before you encircle me and
rest your hand upon me.
If I take the wings of dawn and dwell
beyond the sea,
Even there your hand guides me,
your right hand holds me fast.
If I say, "Surely darkness shall hide me,
and night shall be my light—
Darkness is not dark for you,
and night shines as the day.
Darkness and light are but one.

You formed my inmost being;
you knit me in my mother's womb.
I praise you, because I am wonderfully made;
wonderful are your works!
My very self you know. My bones are not hidden
from you,
When I was being made in secret,
fashioned in the depths of the earth.
Your eyes saw me unformed;
in your book all are written down;
my days were shaped, before one came to be.
How precious to me are your designs, O God;
how vast the sum of them!
Were I to count them, they would outnumber
the sands;
when I complete them, still you are with me.